MUTE HOUSE

...a gentle gravity borne of its palpable
seriousness of purpose. — *Poetry London*, 2015

...the poet himself burrow[s] deeper and deeper,
determined to get at not just the truth of his subject but
its unique and defining features. — *Lunar Poetry*, 2017

From weird hitchhikers to playground lore, from a
caravan park to the wild Pacific, these punchy, slant
poems 'set loose life' in all its brilliant contradictions.
— Helen Mort

GALE BURNS
MUTE HOUSE

EYEWEAR PUBLISHING

POETRY

First published in 2018
by Eyewear Publishing Ltd
Suite 333, 19-21 Crawford Street
Marylebone, London W1H 1PJ
United Kingdom

Cover design and typeset by Edwin Smet
Cover photograph by Gale Burns (Newport Estuary, Pembrokeshire)

Printed in England by TJ International Ltd, Padstow, Cornwall

The right of Gale Burns to be identified as author of
this work has been asserted in accordance with section 77
of the Copyright, Designs and Patents Act 1988
ISBN 978-1-912477-23-4

WWW.EYEWEARPUBLISHING.COM

For Jules and Cheryl Burns

Gale Burns is a writer-in-residence at
Kingston University London and Sydenham Arts Festival.
In 2017, he was presented with an award from the Indjija
International Literary Festival in Serbia; he has been
commended in *Magma*, Poetry Meets Politics and Battered Moon
competitions, and was recently a Hawthornden Fellow. He
convenes the long-running Shuffle poetry series at the Poetry
Cafe, London, and is Vice-President of the European Association
of Creative Writing Programmes. He is one of the founding
members of *Quadrat*, a poetry and climate change website.
Gale has published three pamphlets and his work has been
translated into French (for the Sorbonne's
Place de la Sorbonne), Arabic, Slovenian,
Serbian and Romanian.

TABLE OF CONTENTS

NEAR

FAR

KNOWING

Is it possible, a soft
landing for civilisation?

Michael McKimm, from *Fossil Sunshine*

Ancestors' arrowheads
are still quivering

Ko Un, from *Pride, First Person Sorrowful*

NEAR

ENGLAND

Turn left at the garage with squat pumps rusting,
past the village shop, only one left now – Mrs Dalton
the only news point; past the new vicarage –
the old one, sold – where the vicar lives with his
young male friend. You'll see the village school
with its single class and the churchyard, your ancestors
gently waiting. You pass through manorial gates
under the Downs and there before you, in fields
like rolling seas are three great cedars. Here,
regal horses swish their tails and nod, while noisy rooks
picket the dead elms, speckled with mistletoe,
exploding.

THE HOUSEKEEPER

After au pair upon au pair,
one pregnant, another violent,
Mrs Jay appeared – what was her first name?
She baked floured potatoes and ironed
with rasp-edged humour
and fag from which ash fell.
'Never thought I'd reach forty!' she said,
and so she lived *our* lives,
ignoring the Jungian hush.
Together, we braved adult movies –
'Probably good for him,' mother surmised
and of an evening I would 'shipwreck
in her thighs', leaning back to watch
the missile crisis, the death of Kennedy,
Hanratty's justice. Her heart was saved
for the witless Cocker we bought her,
walking the dog in wild winds – at risk
the hairpiece we never mentioned
and the swollen joints, arthritic
'from jumping in the Arctic'.
My mother died and Mrs Jay
baked floured potatoes and ironed
for the step-father remaining,
until finally she could walk no more.
Her distant daughter descended,
stealing her to dogless Essex.
I saw her once, in a rail terminal.
I did not thank her, or become emotional.
We greeted her family at the funeral,
strangely outnumbered. Mrs Jay:
housekeeper, *sans* house,
borrowed, returned.

WHAT WE LEARNED IN PLAYGROUNDS:

the mystery of public space, unfettered.
How adults do not rule everywhere.
An affinity for airstrips and roads;

the taste of asphalt, sucked from wells.
Of soulmates, hanging off railings with Paul
from the orphanage – then one day he was gone.

Of swirling gangs, led by those who'll later lead
the country. Of weather, how it's *good for you*,
its puddle contours; how to yearn for a radiator.

The worrying fatness of thighs on benches;
the strangeness of girls, their games of hair
and rope we once dared ourselves play.

Dark rumours of menstruation. Of refuge
from forced semolina. The partitions of age;
how to be victim, how then to perpetrate.

EXCEAT CARAVAN PARK

Forced holidays in a box,
sleeping head to toe with my sister,
reliable rain on an aluminium roof.

In sight: a serpent of freshwater, its beguiling
undulations, frothy edge and squadrons of shrimp
protected by stagnation.

Children's hour: rocks moved, velvet anemones clench.
A spindling crab; fish jolt forward, all engulfed
by the torrent flood, our toes washed like stones.

We breathe its spray, study expelled offerings
of bladder wrack, bottles, rope, and cuttlefish bones,
carried inland to build up budgerigars.

The vast level of sea, un-still, unfathomed;
we shrink at its moods, returning each year
to sleep in its thunder beat.

WOODSIDE

You wake at the top of the house to the glow of curtains,
the sun shining over the Downs, the crows caw
from the Pines; you descend the oak stairs to the door
that leads to the porch and the thin sand lawn,
each blade with its globe of dew, each molehill a war.
The Camellia with stripes of red and white is in flower
as if forever, and below in the garden of veg Mr Knight
beams like an imp, ready to tell you the stories
of Lavington Stud. He has come from his cottage, no water
or light, to work in the grounds. The News blares out,
Grandfather cupping his ear to the box as you mark
with tread the virgin lawn, out past the Orangery
where oranges have never been grown, to the wooden gate,
its grain layered with lichen, the fence kept high to hold back
the deer. You escape to the woods, each step a breaking of twigs,
and for this week alone you move between bluebells,
out past the fading magnolia, its petals decaying like cups.
Here, Granny will sit with easel and paint. You climb the hill;
at its crest the great Cedar, planted the year of Grandfather's
birth, and the circular pond of brick, its water drained
to inches, yet teeming with life, newts slipping
into the silt, and the odd brown fish that might turn to gold.
You take from your pocket a book, nothing weighty,
a tale of upper-class mores, and glance at the porch
where the family comes and goes. And you know,
with the tree at your back, that this is as safe
as you'll be; as close as you'll come to a home.

THE LAST HAPPY EATER IN THE SOUTH

I see it against the dusk: a squat box,
red and yellow neon, curtainless windows,
copper-domed lights over tables. In a corner

a biker in black leather chaps chews his
all-day breakfast. From a room in the back
there are giggles, pans crash, someone cries.

Through swing doors 'Mavis' appears
holding a pad – all of fifteen with spots
that drop to her dimple breasts.

Forty years ago I chose; who says
the English have no food? –
rubbery pancakes, and from a tin

viscous cherries with a slab of pale
ice cream that refuses to melt.

SUMMER AT THE WIMPY

The pictures of food are glorious, are love.
The pavement plastic cone could melt.

I'm in company: characters juggle change,
consult themselves in careful choice,

speaking as if they have one line in a
Shakespeare play, by which they are revealed:

Mega-burger, Eskimo Waffle, International Grill.
Fans strobe the glare, fluorescent lights

in a world of a hundred suns. Songs wail
from speakers, a fly swerves from chip to chip.

The ice cream machine, its work done,
will be drained. Behind the glass, fish,

bought to beguile the young, heave the aqueous,
watching moment by moment this theatre of air.

LAYING TURF AROUND THE POND

We work the ground, risen up
and covered in sores. The pond is held
by wishfulness, the apples slung
so low they bob in water.

The small fish twist and turn,
gulp at air; they know little
of our free-fall – how unheld
we are, swathed in skin.

Then rain falls as if through a sieve,
closing the hinge of the day;
as if to announce your leaving,
footsteps marked with gold.

With plants, you can guess intention.
To be with another is a fine-spun thing.

GARDEN

Under the virgin willow, as branches wave
like new-grown hair, the old leaves mulch below.

The conifers are worn, have brazened winter;
the pear will soon be refulgent with bloom.

Long before the scything sycamore throws its seeds
to battle, before the apple bloats like a laden cow,

before we think of Summer as passing, the iris
unbolts, its parts splayed bare.

The pond has seen the jelly eggs of Spring make
multitudes of tadpole serpents, now to the depths

or to the mouths of fish; no more diving frogs,
belching bubbles like a boiled kettle.

Into this, the builder comes and digs a hole
so deep even the foxes are amazed.

They play in the spoils at night, roll in the dirt,
yelping like soldiers ahead of dog wars.

I view the bastard weeds and grass.
With my new mower, I make my move.

HITCHHIKING

Some splurge their stories, others go about
their business. A few take me on their dash
through life, barely avoiding oncoming vans.

Sometimes a woman driver alone will brave
her fear – once becoming a kind of love
on the grass mound of a service station.

Some are just weird: a trucker proposing
an act of sex, then letting me down
into the blackest night.

And the king of rides:
flying above the forests of Ontario –
in the wrong direction.

But mainly there's the waiting:
the counting of cars, the cursing,
the longing for a decoy girlfriend.

To give yourself to strangers, a rite of age,
like the vacuum shock of that first kiss;
like the pay packet with bizarre numbers,

or the cold forehead of a dead parent –
testing if the world can bear me, or I
can bear the world.

THE HIPPIES WERE LONG GONE

Sporting hair to our shoulders, we weighed
the world over brown rice, paid homage
to Monty Python in Common Rooms,

tried to look like Che Guevara, with whiskers curled.
We would sleep with anyone, were anyone interested;
would take drugs, were they not so depressing.

We sneered at those who dined at High Table
and gave degrees to dictators. We studied car workers –
their journeys to work the main skill of their day.

We lauded the youth from town, knew no-one
with children, yet stormed the Senate for a crèche –
making our debut on Police Super 8.

We had posters declaring 'Keep the Dialectic Open'
showing women with their legs wide.
We were rarely alone and often lonely.

We had history – Vietnam, Flower Power,
Garden House, and we hoped, how we hoped
for an Indian Ashram, free love and an Afghan coat.

SUBURBIA

Beds of red roses are turfed. TV boxes become
nests for bantams, injected to stop the crowing.
Concrete is all: patching the trees, building walls
so my trains can tour the shrubs on rusting rails.

One brother builds the family dream – a pool,
waist-high, where hedgehogs dive and die.
I keep pigeons – white fantails, and 'racers' that might
win me twenty pounds – breeding into piebald birds.

We clutter rooms. The eldest claims the attic,
testing girls to the wail of Joan Baez.
My stepfather, besotted with GB Shaw,
has double-doors fitted, brings his book to meals.

My sister is everywhere – for choice enthroned
before coral fires. My teenage brother sinks
pints of milk, belches, and shouts at my mother:
'I didn't ask to be born!'

The shared front garden is patrolled by boys
of civil servants; timid Mr Lawrence
is heard bellowing through walls; all males
yearn for a glimpse of trainee nurse Alice Jay.

When my mother dies, one by one
we go our ways, scornful of suburbia.
But we seek houses with the same-sized rooms
and gardens grand enough for pools.

CRYSTAL PALACE PARADE

Each Tuesday, climbing the road
to the plateau, scoured by sky,

one week, the girders of its Tour d'Eiffel,
lost in white.

One week, heart-shaped leaves
speckle the asphalt view.

One week, no dawn,
just traffic-lights pulsing.

One week, Mathew Caley, taking his child to school,
a poem like leaves in his Broca brain.

One week, a camp of circus toys: Ferris wheel,
a dungeon train, spinning floss machines.

One week, a woman crossing: my mother,
many years gone.

One week, entranced by the stillness of trees;
and another, dulled —

the Parade's tone each morning
inclining my day.

One week, walking the green,
finding a swirl of fire-moulded glass

in which you glimpse yourself,
the avenue, the past.

AUNT ESTHER

She knew the shapes and names of grasses,
could read the timing of clouds.
The pig in the wood would listen all ears
for the jangling bucket of slops.
The waiting cows, bursting with cream,
would watch her stride, their uncut hooves
curved to the sky. Even the fish could tell
as she passed. She'd whisper to horses,
ears pricked forward – long and hard
that night the old grey mare leapt the fence
to die on its own in the woods.

BEN

After his death, my father came
and sat on my sister's yellow sofa.

At the hospital, he'd been desperate
to tear the drips from his arms.

He'd revealed at the end, the horrors
he'd agreed to commit in the war;

that my mother was not the innocent party
he'd allowed her to be for years.

On my ninth birthday, he'd sent an American
tin cement truck, whose barrel turned.

He'd told my teenage brother
they could be no more than friends.

How to be male in such a century?
At the least, genetics bound us.

After a tense visit, as I left he looked
right at me: just looked.

MYTH

From the car we saw the stream,
ankle high amongst the trees; drove
over the stone bridge, my mother
saying 'that's where we'd swim when
we were young'. We never stopped,
hurtling on towards the dry city.
Even then I knew that swimming
wasn't possible, did not trust
historical time, thought of it as myth.
Or maybe the river used to swell,
or the towering adults were tiny then.
If you watch at the break of dawn
they could be there, paddling upstream,
the cold stones indenting their feet.

THE KIBBUTZ

The stars had never been so bright as from
the crest of a water tower with Swedish Kristina,
who in the crux of the night declared herself
to be a lesbian, her words rising into dark.
Below was the shuffle of a boundary guard,
his machine gun slung beside his hip,
the same man who found English Rose and I
attempting sex in the warm pool, everything
slippery, unachievable. We earned these hours
by grabbing bulbous avocados, swinging
crop pickers in pursuit of apples, or worst of all,
stepping through housed chickens, extracting
the flattened dead. The settlers had heroic eyes,
some using their rugged demeanour to pick off
Western girls. The children were herded into
dorms – we escapees from nuclear families
not sure if this was a curse or blessing. And then
the missile came, just one, from over the border
into the main square, shattering the lemon tree.

INDIAN SUMMER

Like a late bloom unfurling,
the sun rallies, warming
a starred sky. We've been

hijacked into a golden age,
strolling along leafy streets
smiling, reaping this bonus,

like the surprise passion
with an ex, slipping into my bed,
the boyfriend asleep next door.

SADDLESCOMBE, WEST SUSSEX

A company of black cows drifts east,
their calves in rocking-horse run.

I know this land, the cut of its shrub,
thawed by summer; have held

my lover on its slope of chalk, the sea
at my back. At the crest of the hill,

against clouds, wisps, blurred lines,
families circle and play, unable to grasp

the vista below: entire lives, villages,
histories, laid bare by the absence of sea.

HOMAGE TO RON

Now they're all bankers. The neighbours
from the past are gone, some to the earth,
others to fields where frost bites hard.

The younger ones are grown – large copies
of themselves, bloated with hormones.
The days of the three-legged race to mark

a royal milestone are like sepia, the road
ever since wide open to traffic – except
the year the snow came down so hard

the Jaguar from up the hill slid sideways
into smaller cars. Well, I shouldn't complain;
the houses are full of children, often tethered

to their nannies and fathers nod as they pile
into 4 x 4s. But the wooden shutters from abroad,
the washed bins, leave no space for ghosts:

the rarely sober Denis, who six months before death
spent his savings gutting the front garden
to park off-street; Eve, who only stopped her speech

to take a breath, and Ron, dear Ron, the most
temperate man alive. I'm the strange one now;
I'm the one they whisper about as I pass by.

EARLY DAYS

We were all white, mainly Jews –
even I with a touch of the Torah –
except for a tall African man
several years ahead, a Prefect,
with stubble on his upper lip
like a fungus that needed long
staring, and a friend Ashwin –
Ashwin Pandit. We'd walk up
Rotherhithe Road from the station,
past his house, talking of nothing
memorable; he'd cross
the crazy paving path, the door
opening, and disappear into
darkness, strange adults manoeuvring,
maybe a turban, the smell of curry
wafting over tired roses.
Our gang, of which he was part,
that had no name or recognition,
whose members drifted in and out
unaccountably – even then all boys –
would call him 'Ashbin Pancake'.
I don't know what became of him,
why the walks home stopped;
whether he's cleaning out toilets or
running a hospital, but when
I think back to those times I still feel
a pleasantness, a laugh at how clever
we were, how ingenious, and an unease.

GIMBALS

First, brown metallic pills; visits
each week to the man with a large spot.
Christmas, staring at the mantelpiece.

Then, drugged sleep for weeks:
dreams stacked upon each other;
shuffles in the ward, unopened cards.

Next, fifty minute hours, a solid room;
road clatter, a green banker's lamp,
a cotton wool hush.

Not forgetting the forced clamping
to the bed, mouth guard, soft pads
to the head – juddering spasms.

At last, home: baked beans, cold
handshakes, footsteps to and from work
avoiding the pavement cracks – rituals

like gimbals of polished brass in a boat
holding the compass level
with their pivots and rings.

VALENTINE'S DAY

It's Valentine's Day, a kind of massacre,
when years ago my mother phones.
She'll watch the News, sleep in their soft bed,
groan in the night, only vaguely heard.
With the seeding of light: a plastic bottle,
a cold forehead, a seep of urine on the sheet.
The New Year of love brings a delegation
to my door. While the body takes its leave
of home, we get to work; I phone friends
with the news, as if delivering a curse.
Then a funeral in the church, where my brother
was married the year before. My uncle wails,
is ushered away; a friend in the pews, at whom
I smile, cannot hold my gaze. The body is laid
so deep to await the husband who will not come.
The yew trees knit their course above the fence,
the carefree horses peering through, the weight
of the Downs up ahead, while here below
we and the muted dead are unable to move.

THE MIDNIGHT GARDENER

When the road is egg-box quiet, my neighbour
scuttles out the back, a hedgehog in the beds.
How he sees I cannot tell, perhaps with touch,
easing the weeds from where they shouldn't be,
slicing the grass with shears. When the moon is up
you'll see his angled back rising and falling
like the working sea, leaving mounds of dark matter
that by the morning are nowhere. When he sleeps
you can't tell, for you can catch him in the day –
he'll smile weakly, squint a little at the sky,
and when you say how fine his garden seems
he'll act surprised, as if it's not his work.
He'll fumble with his hands, but you have seen
the cuts and creases, the soil that's left ingrained.

THE BUILDER

Small, ageing, gimlet eyes, no English;
I serve him tea, four sugars. At first,
we 'sign' my needs; as day blurs
into costly day he's less concerned –

floorboards sanded almost to the joists;
silk white walls, first grey, now black.
Paint smells of him. As thickening dust
covers my browning plants,

corn grows in the kitchen. Some windows
are painted gloss with faint reflection.
Wires now cross the room, crackling.
Shower heads emerge in the bedroom.

The fridge hangs from the ceiling, door
glued shut. I eat wood filler and grout.
He sleeps here now to save time.
The phone rings less; it's always for him.

Often, it *is* him. Sometimes his friends,
all alike, jostle in the hall, but when
they're gone it's too still to breathe.
At night the plaster heaves and sweats.

By morning, like elephant skin, it's grown
an inch. Some walls almost meet.
Floral mouldings have burst in the heat.
My clippings, hair and sperm stuck

to the walls as woodchip. One room is sealed.
At dusk I'm in three rooms at once.
Sometimes I *am* him; small, ageing,
gimlet eyes, no English.

FAR

EUGENE

I'd take the Greyhound bus through darkest oaks
to my Portland love, a Christian who did not believe
in penetration; would float on her pristine flesh to make
a kind of love, as she spoke of Oregon, little else:
its over-grazed Basin Desert, the Bhagwan Big Mud farm,
Route 303 carved along the coast and Eugene –
a town of gentle folk, its glowing women, and men
in rainbow sweaters, still hopeful from the sixties.

Years later, my palms weep as the train slows
into a dusty station, beige, one storey, the sun
shining as in a leafy glade. I'd planned to stop,
my mind already in the imagined high street:
its quaint shops, curly iron lights, whole food cafes.
Eugene holds its breath; my body will not move.
The train slides forward: pulled like a magnet
towards Yosemite, Death Valley, the wild Pacific.

ON MY TEENAGE VISIT TO NY

I didn't leave the flat for days, spying on garbage trucks, taxis, loud horns; only Tuesday going down to the black hobos, living in battered executive chairs, guarding damp books they never sold. You couldn't stand still with the comb of pedestrians. I took refuge in the glaring drug store – buying crisps, Coke, magenta nail varnish – queuing behind Britney, who smiled. We could have been friends had she been there Wednesday. That was when I saw my first naked man, clutching his beer, dancing between cars, his thing flapping. By Thursday, I risked a side street: endless shops selling split rainbow underwear and all number of weed contraptions; Cornelius St Café, where years later I would read poetry; an all-night diner, with resting prostitutes, clients at different tables; and a frozen yoghurt shop, many flavours – Blueberry, Chewing Gum, Baltimore Surprise – even Garbage. It was only Friday I turned a corner to see the oaks of Washington Square with Judson Church in the North. I'd been in the middle of Greenwich Village: Allen Ginsburg, the Black Panthers, Steve Paxton; in the middle of History.

EVERETT, MA

Through the windows of the Cultos di Igreja on Church St,
believers sing to God with upstretched arms.

The Everett Savings Bank on Main Street resembles L'Arc de Triomphe,
and the 24/7 TV proclaims far-off rip tides.

The *Leader Herald News Gazette* headlines Representative Stat Smith
filing legislation to keep the pools open in the record heat.

A man rummages through a waste bin, looks up and smiles.
The *News Gazette* offices display the obit of Joanna M. Cafasso, at 97,

entering into rest from the Chelsea Jewish Nursing Home, active in
the Sons of Italy and the Italian Women's Social Club, and *often seen*

around the family funeral home during wakes and funerals –
with Frederick E. Cafasso, Funeral Counsellor, handling the funeral.

At the bottom of the page, next to Salvatori Rocco and Sons
Funeral Home Inc., a large box ad for Frederick Cafasso and Sons,

founded by the late beloved husband, Members of the Forethought Network
of Funeral Professionals – Funeral Planning Before the Need Arises.

PARIS

A crash at Chatelet: a motorcyclist stares
at heaven. At last, he blinks.

Before Notre Dame, a globe of glass slides
over a juggler's skin. He moulds to its view.

The chestnut trees are clipped square.
The leaves filter the breeze.

A family takes shifts to beg in the street,
their pitch a bomb-blast of clothes.

Below me, the Metro with its glowing belly
hurtles round curves.

A drunk has made his home in the alcove
of the office furniture shop, lit by an Anglepoise.

In a cafe, a could-be star of some French film
talks fiercely of an outrage I almost understand.

This city, confides an Italian friend,
has made me forget spontaneity.

LA COLLE SUR LOUP

It was here for the first time I knew
my mother would one day die.

What to do with such knowledge?
Except fight the gaining heat,

retreat to a siesta covered by cotton.
The grasses singed the air, everything bleached

but the undergrowth and a shuttered lounge.
My family, released from the milk-mild North

lay on baking sands sprayed with salt, or inland
watched Pétanque balls stand in dust

until they'd scorch your skin. Later, we'd walk
to the square, past a field opening –

days of harvest Van Gogh had surely painted
the week before; in the distance, the hill town

of St Paul de Vence. We dined al fresco with
white bread and vine-leaf shadows on skin.

SIESTA

A car starts and remembers
an elsewhere. The sun glows
from stone. The almost asleep
rattle the streets; some hide
behind shutters or in dark shops.
What can be known
is endless days like these,
and the trickle of water
from the mouth of the stone face
on the church wall.

WALKING THE RIVER AT TIMISOARA

Maybe on a Sunday stroll like this
she'll choose and life will change
its course again; the wind will blow
from West to East not East to West,
and he'll adopt the oddness of her world,
all he can see, the folds of time
will manifest as this, embracing
all, were he to be embraced.
So now they walk in bleach and shadow,
walking the remedy, until the night
when all is black and folk let loose
their dreams upon a licit world.
The sky is up, the earth below;
they're in a country of their making.

NEWPORT

The seagull at the window holds quite still.
The single road through town is packed,
stragglers from a bygone age, shuffling past.
We inhabitants of now, with our graces,
think ourselves immune. Christmas lights
zag across the road. My one true love
(would that she were) whispers at the air.
By the church, children mass, all heights, insist
on being heard – we have not ruined them yet.
Across the estuary sands, voices, a tone so clear
that some men weep and women sigh. The old,
who have been cynical to date, seem pleased.
The Second Coming is perhaps like this:
not a single thing, but many, altogether.

MALMÖ

I carve my name in the foam seat – immortal
for a while. The man with the scarred head
sighs: I see his thoughts. I give the book
in a strange tongue to the waitress who dances
from table to table. She repays me with tea
that I carry away and pass to a beggar who
hints at a smile. Give away your golden bars,
your inhaled air, your cherished thoughts,
heard by you in the core of the night as dawn
prepares to announce itself oh so subtly
you have rumours of its coming: the birds
ruffle their feathers, their throats quiver.
You turn to your loved one, still asleep as if forever
and hum in a tone unheard of in the day, so that
she dreams as if she floats on quilt of the man
with a scared head, who, thank god, is happy.

BRIEFING FOR WINTER

Imagining cold.
Leaves

make the longest journey.
Fog breath.

Poplars
loosening gold.

Hearsay of Christmas:
foliage red in alarm.

Fruit outside shops,
chilled.

Cotton gives way to wool.
Gasps of blue sky,

the world, skeletal.
Then from the North,

polar scrapings,
stark stars.

WOODS

There are flowers — primroses, bluebells,
wild orchids — the great seducers,

and without warning, rain; one
of its thirty forms — mist-film, long-trail, near-ice;

when gone, the gentle snapping of twigs.
The dandelion domes have shattered frames.

Even the river is rain, fighting back
with froth against the flow.

At the heart of the wood, in a furnace cage,
a branch is scorched to the bone.

The sun is weak. I ponder the benignness
of woods when a deer erupts, lopes away,

and stopping, turns full-square.
I am seen, as nowhere else,

as a woodland beast. At will, like a baby,
she looks aside and is gone.

The midges weave their corps de ballet.
A mosquito makes its jagged run.

MÉNAGE

He was in a loveless ménage a trois with a French woman manager, whose son spent his days lost on drugs, but whose houseplants flourished, the leaves glistening. Her cleaner came once a week at indeterminate times, often putting her feet up on the settee; she had an elderly mother lying like a foetus in the local hospital, 'blocking' a bed that three were waiting for in the corridor, one a breeder of rabbits, who was worried they wouldn't be watered, their pellets growing harder and harder until the rabbits were desiccated – too *maigre* for the local restaurant, mainly vegetarian, but that made exceptions for the older customers the owner inherited; they hardly had the teeth for meat but persisted from stubbornness – one a past ballet dancer, who still performed in her front room, with its three chairs, to invited guests. Her main ambition was no longer theatrical, but was to join her sister in the ménage a trois, or better still replace her or one of its members, thereby keeping its name and bringing love to a heretofore practical arrangement.

ONE DAY

One day you'll get a call: you'll think it's from God, but
he's otherwise engaged. More likely from a childhood
friend, a window on your murky past you've learnt
to hide, more so now your bedridden mother forgets
everything bad in your life and hers, like the time the
heavens opened and rained down gold, or so we thought:
Saharan sand, scouring paint and skin.

'Answer the damn phone,' your crazy wife shouts, not
knowing she's on the way out, maybe in days, because
you've a friend, someone downstairs, who treats you
kind. 'We marry our mothers', they say, but mine is
something else; I had to marry several – all pictured at my
last wedding, furious at me and each other.

Sometimes I want sex with the ex; often they'll oblige,
but some won't give it up unless there's a ring on their
finger – any ring will do. The phone rings. 'You waiting
for God to answer the damn thing?' she yells.

RINGSTEAD BAY

We boated wildly, peering over wooden rims
to glacial pools, rainbow fish sliding into view.

Everything panned before us; walls bleached
by sun, a heavy throat of sea, countless adult legs.

The path between the pines marked an elsewhere.
If we could've foretold what such days would precede

as we dug and patted boats from sand,
our pride caught by the family Brownie,

and mused at gangs of reef men, hunting octopi
we never saw, their fabled plumes of ink,

their sucking arms that hugged you
till you drowned.

MY NEIGHBOUR MOOSE

Who knows why Moose bays?
Maybe to shake the leaves of trees,
or to guide incoming waves;
maybe for some lost bitch on which
his hopes were hitched.
He bays in the creases of the day;
nothing will stop him, this his calling –
in another life a cantor, a muezzin.
We met once, his Labrador hackles raised,
stood down by his redneck master.
Now he bays as if in tongues, as if
the world's troubles had reached him,
and the pain of existence was a sound.

LUNCH WITH NIKKA

Nikka sleeps in the room downstairs where her daughter
and I eat omelette and cheese. Two Indian men

with stubbly beards come and test the motion sensor;
the night carer can tell if Nikka gets up.

The carers' supervisor calls; the daughter reads each word
of the contract: *It's the dog that's aggressive, not my mother.*

Nikka, in photos, has languorous legs and a seen-it-all smile
that must have lured my father.

Aged 14, she'd pleaded with the Gestapo to let them go
to the West. *In a home, they'd tie her to a chair to keep her upright.*

My father wanted to die for months. As I look at the daughter,
I see him, with eyebrows long beyond reason.

So Nikka – Lithuania, Germany, then Canada, now absent
among the Jews of Edgware, maybe dreaming, maybe

robbed of even this, ready to wake at five. But we are gone.
My half-sister and I are wheeling the old wicker basket

brimming with mismatched crockery to the Station Road
charity shop, and not a piece has been broken. Not one piece.

ANNIHILATION

All praise for the almost unknown Stanislav Petrov,
a Russian, last year dead at the age of 77.

He detected missiles fired from American soil
but couldn't move. *I felt like I was sitting on a frying pan.*

Twenty-five minutes to annihilation, with a strange feeling
in his gut, he failed to tell the high command and Andropov,

but instead reported a malfunction. There are people
such as this. All praise to his mum and dad, who maybe

raised him to be calm, to think for himself. The satellite
had mistaken the sun's reflection off the top of the clouds

for Armageddon. At first, he was celebrated,
then admonished for failing to record events precisely.

I had a phone in one hand and the intercom in the other,
he responded. *I don't have a third hand.*

ON THE MOVE

Budapest Station 2015

And so our journey begins, the clanking train
taking us far from what we knew and did not love,
from a station of concrete and wires, selling kaftans,
trainers, bangles – almost nothing you'd need
for a journey. The windows are jammed or locked,
the glass is layered with dust; we're seated
in square compartments where no-one
would find a lifelong friend or love,
but you learn to speak to strangers,
a funeral calling for one, a new world for others;
who would be trembling with anticipation
were this not forbidden, for there is no actual sign
but we know the rules of pleasant conversation.
You examine the scenes of countryside flying past
and imagine a life where all trains stopped
on tracks that simply ceased, where we stepped
down that long great reach onto the shingle stones,
nowhere a sign of water, nowhere an inn to lure you,
just field after field, the local people shut indoors,
the train for years rumbling past with not so much
as a wave and here we are, the wooded hills
far off, too far to reach unnoticed.

KNOWING

THE TASTE OF HORSE,

its scurf, packed under your nails;
its barrel weight, pinning you to a stable wall;
its kick, enough to snap a bone;

its spurt of piss, almost sweet, attended
by flurrying girls; its scorched hooves,
rasped, branded with glowing steel;

its sedate walk, letting loose droppings
of packed grass – Rye, Dropseed, Muhly;
its trot, jolting canter, and floating gallop;

its drenched flanks after a hunt, oblivious
to the quarry, running with its own will –
maybe in flight from horsed wars.

You look to its opal eye and see
nothing: no flicker, just the distant
horizon line, the long-lost plain.

WHALE SONG

One hundred whales, on asylum from the sea,
glistening beans, poached in sand.

Did they dream? Did I wail to pull them in?
Like ancient fishes, they claim the land.

Their fins sail, halfway to flight
– whole pods of whales on suicide pact.

We shroud them in towels and whisper *Hold on!*
I charge the water to beckon them back.

One hundred whales – we and they beached.
Perhaps they'll sing the weeds of deep.

THE WORM

No eyes, no mouth or gut;
a prince of dark, stretched
seven metres long,
clamped to mucosa;
a crown of thorns
with which to claim its place –
my snug gut-mate,
wriggling at whim,
ecstatic at self-sex.
I, growing thin, eat for ten,
provide a masticated stream.
I am its moods. Through
nights and blurry days
it sings out
procreate.
Now we make our dream:
we set loose life.

THE WIND

We barred and battened windows, watching debris
sweep before us – the garden table, brittle branches,
flightless birds – the cat gripped to a post.

At midday, slapped like new-borns,
we tilt against the blast, never breathing so deeply;
envied trees whose roots could grip the soil.

But then my friend thrusts her body into the slipstream:
she twirls and loops until she is the wind. I see her smile,
her shrinking form pulled to the distant vortex.

THE WARMING

Mosquitos swarm on a winter's day,
cockroaches crawl from cooker and bed,
black bubble ants zigzag gaps
of sky – only our dreams free of them.

Then the gritty storms bring locusts,
a few at first. Jane, excited, calls them
regal grasshoppers. They hew the shoots
and vegetables to shreds.

Next, flying machines dive and bore the skin;
by night and day, we're veiled. I knew
of their coming: risen from our desire, our oil,
our heat, given brittle leg and wing.

The old mediations – boric acid, heptachlor,
DDT – seem puny, poisoning us within.

THE COX

Before the sun exists,
in a land of stumbling shapes
I raise myself, pulled

by an agreement
and an unmarked river
which we carve.

As light blurts the horizon
the bow spurts,
an impossible insect, parallel legs.

Eight men with naked thighs
heave back, stirring private pools.
Their scent and sweat stream by,

I am mascot, queen, cripple.
My puny size has weight,
my will, muscle.

Mist hangs between stunted trees.
I hunch forward,
the world speeds by.

IN THE SHED,

a chorus of breath, like a mosque
in prayer, a shuffle of hard hooves,

a churn of jaws; mound upon mound
of haunch, velvet-wrapped;

the arch of a back, a firing cough
that shoots behind.

Some moan with the bulge of slung calves,
their black eyes vacant.

Your hand on a flank, you work
to tease the fluid white – drips,

then spurting on stone; you, the gatherer,
the Cuckoo-calf, the thief.

THEFT

I walk into another man's house
and steal his life, his gotten gains.
I like to think he's evil, but it's not true,
no worse than you or I – the wrong
man in the wrong place, caught
by something he won't understand.
I strike a winning pose. His wife and daughter
meet the change, reluctantly at first,
but now they see the point of someone
fresh and something new. There're
many things he failed to do: the hinge
rusting on the garden gate, the odd
kind word, the finding of the sweet spot that
would make her squirm; the daughter too.
All things change. His office was less keen;
they'd meetings to discuss the shift,
debated right and wrong, but they grew
weary. I now claim his desk, his secretary
to boot, who sometimes straddles my knee
and tells me just how life's improved.
His family are welcoming as if I were
their own – they even talk of baby tales
and teenage pranks they might have seen.
But I grow tired; maybe I desire the change
and not the life. A man I talked to on the train
intrigues me, his haughty air. What's his wife
like in the sheets; what might he dream?

THE PITCH

The cricket pitch lies ready. The iron roller
has done its task. Fathers and sons have trod
this turf for years, have stood with ragged hats
in wavering heat, suffered both the elation
and the rout. But this is the drought year.
Across the green a fissure zags from east to west
– nothing has ever been seen like this before.
Wise men are rushed from pubs, they suck
their cheeks, ponder 'Is this the end of Summer?
Or even sport?' – the nearby football pitch
untouched, but here a gash enough to sink
three balls or fielders' feet. Some pray in church,
confessing wrongs, some consider their infidelities,
others give up drink for days. Yet still the fissure
gapes, baring its earth like a chasm. So the men
decide to tend the grass, to talk of cricket as though
the season would soon be hastened. No matter
that no over had been played, nor would be.

LOVE

So this: the architecture of love, a chapel
of ribs and triangles; a waking in the night
to what was left undone.

And when the morning comes, as come
it must, how bright is even the greyest day,
how tall the trees, how mute the houses.

COMMITMENT

The lover before you could make me smile.
I list your imperfections; you list mine.

AUTUMN WAS A WEEK;

For SW

the leaves fell and kept on falling.
Then it rained so hard the water rose
above the earth, a kind of benediction.

In the local ward, her spine crumbled.
She shrank, like her mother before her,
yet fought the fight she always fought.

This is the way we go: some harbouring
a growth for years, others caught afresh.
These are the stories, not yet told.

AFTER DEATH

After the troubled talk of offspring,
after the anguished night,
the struggle to do the simplest things –
to take a breath, to say a phrase,

lct alone hold yourself to account.
After the close of lids, the drain of skin,
the washing of the body –
the head tilted back

towards the door, open-mouthed.
After the misted dawn has filtered
into the room; after the relief
of a kind, for days we would see

inert bodies in passers-by; imagine
their corpses not at peace.

HOSPITAL

The fitter explains how they *run some pipes to destruction*;
he prefers *planned preventative maintenance*.

The consultant with bow tie leads his goslings
to the workers' café.

Gangs of fresh medics loiter, ghosts of my parents,
who learned while bombs fell on London.

A friend, to keep her alive, was put in an armchair
and given poison.

Would Patrick McGoohan turn the corner, chased
by a bouncing orb?

How do you get a trophy stethoscope? A family
takes the passageway ride to the wards.

I walk the corridors, trying to guess the conditions.
The man who probed my gut nods again when we pass.

THE UNFORGIVING

The apples hang on trees without a leaf.
I am rain, glistening in the streets.

The cherry in full bloom is out of season.
I am water, that can only flow downhill.

In the rooms of the departed the eldest son
has gone, his playthings stacked.

I learn to read the pavement leaves.
Love has left us – so much wanted.

THE MOURNER

I set out my dark suit and tie,
pressed shirt, raven socks, cufflinks.
I look at the schedule, plot the best route.

I like this work: no prospects or chat.
I'm not an emotional man, but feel for
the sick and the dead – they owe us nothing.

To the crematorium or church, an undertaker, a vicar,
a body, and me – three pews back. A life of
encounters and loves, no family or friends –

sometimes refusing to bury them, sometimes
pre-deceased or dredged from lakes, unknown.
I can be moved, yes, for the little we know of them,

for a world where souls can die alone
into the hands of God and the municipal authorities,
into the hands of the Mourner, your unknown friend.

BARABBAS

No one gives a child my name;
for me no manger, no chorus of beasts.

'One of the guys'; a cheeky smile,
a way with the crowd.

Some say I stole, others a brigand,
a leader of the uprising.

We were both rebels, but I did more
than preach. The son of God, water to wine!

My life went on; my story stopped.
Some think of me as Christ, others

blame me for the nails. But the cross
made him. No INRI on my death.

I'm Jesus Barabbas – the escape artist,
the bit part, the patron saint of thieves.

TOWARDS A COMPENDIUM OF HUMAN CONDITIONS

CONDITION XVIII MELANCHOLY

Although this state possesses the sonic chimes of the cauliflower family, this most serious of human conditions can lead to inaction or sudden death if not identified in the morning. While there is no known cure, the simple identification of the condition appears to be a relief to all concerned, including even the victim. Its genesis is as yet undetermined, but controlled trials in animals as diverse as the Rhesus Monkey and the Hard-Winged Beetle (who appear to exhibit melancholia by walking backwards in circles) point to some chemical imbalance, which can in both instances be exacerbated by the over-consumption of mushrooms. Similar effects have been shown in humans, which calls into question the current controversial treatment of attempting to initiate a response through humour, or in severe cases, any response at all.

CONDITION XXXVII HAPPINESS

This is happily a rare condition and is often confused with noisy, disruptive behaviour, rhythmic lung action and a certain unpredictability. Scientists have now been able to replicate the sensations alloyed to the condition with the help of artificially produced chemicals, many of which can be taken voluntarily without the need for institutionalisation.

The exact purpose of this state, after some research, is still unclear, although some professional attempts to calibrate a standard of variation has recently proved possible with the German HPS Index. Unfortunately, this does rely on a high degree of self-assessment, and scientists are not convinced that this has much validity in the establishment of its dimensions. Some even question its very existence, using the term 'merely aspirational'. Others are more sanguine.

CONDITION XX DEATH

This is a confusing condition in that in order to perceive its dimensions it does not seem possible to inhabit its experience and make a report. It nevertheless appears to be a condition about which there is much cerebral activity and remarkably little knowledge. Occasionally individuals maintain they have been victims of the condition and then recovered, but the evidence can be viewed as somewhat unreliable.

Some cells in humans, as in other life-forms, seem to replicate themselves ad infinitum, giving rise to the speculation that death is part of the process of aiding this replication.

Experiments have taken place over the years on a massive scale, and yet, this does not seem to have pushed forward the boundaries of knowledge.

77

On other pages, conditions include SUPERIORITY, AMNESIA, ITCHINESS, SELF-LOATHING, POETITIS, LOATHING OTHERS, DISINTEREST, and more.

BETWEEN THE TREES

for Ko Un

I open my window to parallel lines.
I love these lines; I watch them grow.

Should a woman appear, my children
will play between them.

The man who sired me does not know
my name. My siblings come, I can't tell why.

They say I do not understand the world,
but I have seen the traders come and go.

I'm told of all the things being done by men,
yet I've done none. In the land of the innocent

all are guilty. The priest told me how to pray.
From where I am it's hard to fall from grace.

The man who built this hut was sad:
he dripped acid in his ear.

As autumn comes, the trees will turn —
never a single leaf, but many altogether.

THE DENOUEMENT

They that are terribly known, the loveless, who inhabit this space,
this borough, whose culmination brought us to this point,

their reputation preceding them as ours did not, whose blight
upon the city squares and walls, whose terror in the night –

the barking dogs, the screams that turn you blue – they wake us;
yet who these miscreants are you couldn't tell, some wondering

if they did exist at all. Our fears would build, the brain obsessed.
Conferences were held. What would give rise to such amongst our kin?

To grabbers, cutters, snatchers and their sort. Maybe they'd been
dropped when young from some great height? Their deeds are grave,

or so it seemed. Who could save us? Who might venture out at night
to witness or even stop these things? Appeals are made to those

that can enforce the law, but many speak of secret deals and wads
of cash that suddenly appear for no good reason. Some harangue

the leaders of the state. Perhaps incompetence has played its part,
enforcers often caught adrift: the time they cuffed a drunk who

cursed too loud and let a gangster free, his orbit much enhanced.
What can be done? Just when we thought a denouement might not

come, we found a go-between from their bleak past, an interlocutor,
a dapper man in a cold grey suit who never stops his smile.

SABBATH

It is the Sabbath, when the Hasidim refuse
to flick a switch and even shops have closed by two.
The dying see if they can hold till Sunday,
a short time further, and maybe for a week or month
for who can tell the body's machinations with
the healing power of God, who whispers in our ears
'Your work is far from over' – this we know, of course,
even we who never knew the nature of the work
or its dimension, for we have carried the incomplete
for all our lives and what we thought was done
has not been done at all. What is the message
of the human? Noble in parts, of noble aspiration,
and yet an arrogance, a bending to our will of all
that we can see, but more than that, a cacophony
of sound: the soundscape of the human.
In which we're lost, like a child set free in some
terrain with little guidance – she hums the tune
she learnt at four with all her might, as if the tune
might save her, the sun and sand her parents now.

THE WOOD TURNER

Hardly a stretch of skin without a crease,
tufts of hair from every possible place,
cataract eye, flesh just on its frame

and yet before him, an array of the smoothest wood,
the finest grain, burnished with oil and love,
making bowls your fingers ache to touch.

ACKNOWLEDGEMENTS

Some of these poems appeared previously in print
or online in the following places: *Place de la Sorbonne,
Magma*, *The Wolf*, *Battered Moon*, *South Bank Poetry,*
Kuwaiti newspaper *Aljarida,* and *Arte Stih*, Serbia.

Other poems first appeared in anthologies *Poetry Meets
Politics* (Hungry Hill Writing, 2018), *Binsted Poetry Festival
Anthology* (2018), *Indjija International Literary Anthology*
(2017*), 54th Association of Belgrade Writers Anthology* (2017),
Portile Poeziei (Editura TIM Rsita) Romania (2016), *Robin
Hood Book Anthology* (Caparison Press, 2012), *City Lights*
(Tall Lighthouse, 2009), *The Shuffle Anthologies* (The
Shuffle, 2008, 2011, 2011), and *The Unbearable Health of
Being* (Lewisham Hospital, 2008).

Many thanks to Todd Swift, Alex Wylie, and the
Eyewear team, and to guidance from Mimi Khalvati,
Roddy Lumsden, Jacob Sam-La Rose, and Greta
Stoddart. Thanks also to Mona Arshi, Aleš Šteger, Jules
and Cheryl Burns, Hawthornden, and the Slovenian
Writers' Association.

See www.galeburns.co.uk

OO **EYEWEAR** PUBLISHING

TITLES INCLUDE

EYEWEAR
POETRY

ELSPETH SMITH DANGEROUS CAKES
CALEB KLACES BOTTLED AIR
GEORGE ELLIOTT CLARKE ILLICIT SONNETS
BARBARA MARSH TO THE BONEYARD
DON SHARE UNION
SHEILA HILLIER HOTEL MOONMILK
SJ FOWLER THE ROTTWEILER'S GUIDE TO THE DOG OWNER
JEMMA BORG THE ILLUMINATED WORLD
KEIRAN GODDARD FOR THE CHORUS
COLETTE SENSIER SKINLESS
ANDREW SHIELDS THOMAS HARDY LISTENS TO LOUIS ARMSTRONG
JAN OWEN THE OFFHAND ANGEL
SEAN SINGER HONEY & SMOKE
HESTER KNIBBE HUNGERPOTS
MEL PRYOR SMALL NUCLEAR FAMILY
TONY CHAN FOUR POINTS FOURTEEN LINES
MARIA APICHELLA PSALMODY
ALICE ANDERSON THE WATERMARK
BEN PARKER THE AMAZING LOST MAN
MARION MCCREADY MADAME ECOSSE
MARIELA GRIFFOR DECLASSIFIED
MARK YAKICH THE DANGEROUS BOOK OF POETRY FOR PLANES
HASSAN MELEHY A MODEST APOCALYPSE
KATE NOAKES PARIS, STAGE LEFT
U.S. DHUGA THE SIGHT OF A GOOSE GOING BAREFOOT
TERENCE TILLER THE COLLECTED POEMS
MATTHEW STEWART THE KNIVES OF VILLALEJO
PAUL MULDOON SADIE AND THE SADISTS
JENNA CLAKE FORTUNE COOKIE
TARA SKURTU THE AMOEBA GAME
MANDY KAHN GLENN GOULD'S CHAIR
CAL FREEMAN FIGHT SONGS
TIM DOOLEY WEEMOED
MATTHEW PAUL THE EVENING ENTERTAINMENT
NIALL BOURKE DID YOU PUT THE WEASELS OUT?
USHA KISHORE IMMIGRANT
LEAH UMANSKY THE BARBAROUS CENTURY
STEVE KRONEN HOMAGE TO MISTRESS OPPENHEIMER
FAISAL MOHYUDDIN THE DISPLACED CHILDREN OF DISPLACED CHILDREN
ALEX HOUEN RING CYCLE
COLIN DARDIS THE X OF Y
JAMES FINNEGAN HALF-OPEN DOOR
SOHINI BASAK WE LIVE IN THE NEWNESS OF SMALL DIFFERENCES
MICHAEL WILSON BEDLAM'S BEST & FINEST
GALE BURNS MUTE HOUSE
REBECCA CLOSE VALID, VIRTUAL, VEGETABLE REALITY
KEN EVANS TRUE FORENSICS
ALEX WYLIE SECULAR GAMES